Holy Ghost Baptism
An Introduction into the Supernatural
Felix Domrufus

Gifted Anchor Books

Contents

Scripture quotations

T hroughout this book, you'll encounter scriptures primarily
from the King James Version (KJV), with a blend of other
translations such as The Message (MSG), New International Version (NIV), and New Living Translation (NLT).

Dedication

To the Holy Spirit,
Our Comforter, Guide, and Teacher,
The source of wisdom, power, and truth.
Thank You for Your presence and inspiration.
May this book glorify You and draw others closer to Your heart.

Chapter 1

NEW BIRTH EXPERIENCE

The New Birth

A new birth is a supernatural or spiritual experience that takes place in the life of an individual. The word new birth comes from [John 3:3], and the Bible further explains where the birthing takes place, which is in our spirit. So, a new birth is a spiritual birth that occurs in our spirit. It is the rebirthing of our spirit, our spirit coming back to life or becoming alive again.

On account of the fall of man, man was disconnected from God, who is the source of life. Because of this, our spirit lost contact and connection, which led to its death. Death, then, refers to the separation of our spirit from God in this context. This resulted in the loss of man's divine consciousness as well as his inherited dominion, authority, and power over creation. God views death as the end of our relationship with him; hence, we were split off from God as a result of the fall.

Alive in Him

God looked for a way of making us alive by connecting us back to him because a dead being cannot worship and serve him. He achieved this by sending his son in human form to come and die, so the sinful nature that led to our spiritual death would be dealt with. Jesus became sin, and he was crucified on the cross. When the body of Jesus was nailed to the cross, it was actually sin that was nailed to the cross. Jesus bore our sinful nature into his body.

When Jesus resurrected, he resurrected with a new body, which was made alive by the quickening of the holy spirit.

> "But if the Spirit of him that raised up Jesus from the dead dwell in you, he that raised up Christ from the dead shall also quicken your mortal bodies by his Spirit that dwelleth in you" – Romans 8:11 (KJV).

When we believe in what Jesus did for us and confess him with our mouth, he comes into our lives, but by his spirit [Rev 3:20]. His spirit comes in and dwells within us, but the aspect of us that his spirit dwells in is our spirit. Our body becomes his temple [1 Cor 3:16, 6:19].

New birth means the reconnection of our spirit to God through the Holy Spirit, which makes our spirit become alive, recreated, or regenerated. This experience leads to the re-birthing of our human spirit. When the holy spirit comes into us, he gives us the type of life that leads to the resurrection of the body of Jesus because it is the spirit of God that gives life.

"It is the spirit that quickeneth; the flesh profiteth nothing: the words that I speak unto you, they are spirit,
and they are life" John 6:63 (KJV).

The type of life that He gives us is known as God's type of life.
It is this type of life that enables us to live for God because it is
from God, and as a result of it, we are born of God. The Bible
likens this life to a seed; "*Being born again, not of corruptible seed, but
of incorruptible, by the word of God, which liveth and abideth for ever.
For all flesh is as grass, and all the glory of man as the flower of grass.
The grass withereth, and the flower thereof falleth away: But the word
of the Lord endureth for ever. And this is the word which by the gospel
is preached unto you.*" 1 Peter 1:23–25(KJV).

"We know that whosoever is born of God sinneth not;
but he that is begotten of God keepeth himself, and that
wicked one toucheth him not" 1 John 5:18 (KJV).

When our spirit is made alive by the Holy Spirit, we are now able
and worthy to stand before God and worship him.

There are many things that happen at new birth

We are translated into the kingdom of God

"Who hath delivered us from the
power of darkness, and hath trans-

lated us into the kingdom of his
dear Son" Colossians 1:13 (KJV).

At new birth, we are delivered from darkness into light and
was translated into the kingdom of God.

We are begotten of God.

"Whosoever is born of God doth
not commit sin; for his seed re-
maineth in him: and he cannot
sin, because he is born of God" 1
John 3:9 (KJV).

At new birth, we become born of God through his spirit.

We receive the life of God.

"For God so loved the world, that
he gave his only begotten Son,
that whosoever believeth in him
should not perish, but have ever-
lasting life" (John 3:16).

"It is the Spirit that quickeneth; the flesh profiteth nothing: the words that I speak unto you, they are spirit, and they are life" (John 6:63).

At new birth, we receive the life of God through the spirit of God. It is this life that makes us alive to God.

We receive the nature of God.

> "Jesus answered, Verily, verily, I say unto thee, Except a man be born of water and of the Spirit, he cannot enter into the kingdom of God. That which is born of the flesh is flesh; and that which is born of the Spirit is spirit. Marvel not that I said unto thee, Ye must be born again" (John 3:5-7).

Being born again means to be born of the spirit; to be born of the spirit means to be born of God; to be born of God means to have the nature of God within you.

The new birth experience is the foundation of all Christian experiences, because it is at the new birth experience that we become born of God [1 John 3:9] and are introduced into the kingdom of God.

We become new creatures.

> "Therefore if any man be in Christ, he is a new crea-
> ture: old things are passed away; behold, all things are
> become new" 2 Cor 5:17 (KJV).

At new birth, we become new creatures.

We are made citizens of heaven and ambassadors of God.

We are made citizens of heaven and ambassadors of God, and we
gain access to the rights, privileges, and possibilities that are in
God's kingdom.

> The new birth experience opens us up to all other
> spiritual experiences, including the baptism of the Holy
> Spirit. All these experiences enable us to live and func-
> tion like God while on earth.

The Holy Spirit comes to recreate us and make us new in God.
"Not by works of righteousness which we have done, but according to his
mercy he saved us, by the washing of regeneration, and renewing of the
Holy Ghost;" Titus 3:5 (KJV). At this point, our old lives and past
experiences are washed away and forgotten by God.

Chapter 2

DIFFERENT MEASURES OF THE HOLY SPIRIT

T he Holy Spirit comes to us in different measures; there is the operation of the Holy Spirit at salvation, and there is the operation of the Holy Spirit at baptism. Through the word of God, we have an understanding of the different operations of the Holy Spirit.

Salvational Measure

> "Even the spirit of truth, whom the world cannot receive, because it seeth him not, neither knows him, but ye know him, for he dwelleth with you and shall be in you" John 14:17 (KJV).

The Bible says he dwells with us and shall be in us. Dwelling with us means the external manifestation of his presence. The statement "*he shall be in us*" indicates the internal manifestation of his presence, and one of the internal manifestations of the Holy Spirit is salvation.

When a Christian is born again, he receives the measure of the Holy Spirit, which is called the salvational measure. This happens the moment we believe and confess the lordship of Jesus and receive him; automatically, the Holy Spirit tabernacles in us and begins to do an internal work. Some measure of the Holy Spirit definitely dwells in us when we are reborn by our confession.

> "But ye are not in the flesh, but in the Spirit, if so be that the Spirit of God dwell in you. Now if any man have not the Spirit of Christ, he is none of his. And if Christ be in you, the body is dead because of sin; but the Spirit is life because of righteousness" Romans 8:9–10 (KJV).

Baptismal Measure

The baptismal measure of the Holy Spirit will be our cardinal point of discussion. In the book of John 14:17, the bible says that the Holy Spirit will dwell with us, and this is the external or outward manifestation of the Holy Spirit.

There are two kinds of water that Jesus promised:

A well of water springing up into everlasting life

> "But whosoever drinketh of the water that I shall give him shall never thirst; but the water which I shall give him shall be in him a well of water springing up to eternal life.". John: 4:14 (KJV).

Rivers of living water

> "In the last day, that great day of
> the feast, Jesus stood and cried, If
> any man thirsts, let him come unto
> me and drink." John: 7:37 (KJV).

Always remember that the well of water comes before the rivers of living water. So, the well of water speaks about the salvational measure, while the rivers of living water speak about the baptismal measure.

No Salvation, No Baptism

It is salvation that lays the foundation for baptism. There is never a time when an unbeliever is baptized with the Holy Spirit. An unbeliever cannot receive the baptismal measure without receiving the salvational measure. Salvation comes before baptism. Baptism with the Holy Spirit is like an endowment or clothing of power upon a believer to become effective for kingdom service in order for the will of God to be executed. For further understanding about the different measure or dual nature of the Holy Spirit, get my book titled "*The Ministry of the Holy Spirit*".

Chapter 3

UNDERSTANDING BAPTISM

What is baptism?

The Greek word baptizo is the source of the term baptism. Baptizo is from bapto, which means to dip, to overwhelm with, to bury into, and to be immersed, submerged, or washed with water. Even the people of God experienced baptism, according to the instructions given to Moses by God. The New Testament baptism, conducted through immersion, was clearly understood by the ministry of John the Baptist. John's Baptism is not an act of ceremonial purification, which is done by the priest in the book of Leviticus, where the priests were instructed to perform a ceremonial purification in water before and after performing their priestly duties. Rather, it is an act or system of one identifying and coming into a new way of life due to the conviction and decision the person has made. John the Baptist introduced a new way aimed at one's preparation for the kingdom of God that is coming.

The person of Jesus Christ represented the kingdom of God. Anyone who believed John's message was baptized, by submerging the person in the water, which is a physical act that signifies that the person has accepted the new pattern of life that John preached about. This is an outward proclamation of inward conversion. Many people came to be baptized, including the Pharisees and Sadducees, publicans, and soldiers [Matt 3:7, Luke 3:12, 14]. John's baptism is done only when one believes in John's message; his type of baptism is known as the baptism of repentance [repentance, a change of way of life by a change in mindset]. John told the people that he baptized them with water, but one is coming: Jesus, who will baptize people with the Holy Spirit and with fire.

> "I indeed baptize you with water unto repentance, but
> he that cometh after me is mightier than I, whose shoes
> I am not worthy to bear; he shall baptize you with the
> Holy Ghost and with fire" Matt 3:11 (KJV).

John also baptized Jesus in order to fulfill all righteousness; God gave him a sign that whoever has a different encounter during baptism is the same as the Messiah [Jn 1:32–33]. John also baptized Jesus as an act of identifying him as the son of God and an act of ordination.

> "And I knew him not, but that he should make manifest
> to Israel; therefore, I come baptizing with water" John:
> 1:31 (KJV).

Through the ministry of John the Baptist, we see a dimension of water baptism, known as baptism unto repentance. He also revealed another baptism, which is baptism with the Holy Spirit and with fire.

"John answered, saying unto them all, I indeed baptize you with water; but one mightier than I cometh, the latchet of whose shoes I am not worthy to unloose, shall baptize you the Holy Ghost and with fire" Luk 3:16 (KJV).

What Is Baptism With The Holy Spirit?

As we mentioned earlier, baptism means being immersed or submerged in water. Baptism with the Holy Spirit means to be immersed or submerged in the Holy Spirit. It is the outpouring of the Holy Spirit into the life of a believer. When one believes in God and is converted, the Holy Spirit comes in and dwells in their lives; this experience is known as regeneration, and the Holy Spirit lives within that person's life. When the disciple of Jesus was converted, eternal life was given to them, but eternal life entered them through the person of the Holy Spirit.

"And when he had said this, he breathed on them and said unto them, Receive ye the Holy Ghost:" John 20:22 (KJV).

From that point, the Holy Spirit comes in to dwell in them, but Jesus still instructed them to wait in Jerusalem till the Holy Spirit comes upon them [baptism with the Holy Spirit]. Acts 1:4-5

"And behold, I send the promise of my Father upon you: but tarry ye in the city of Jerusalem, until ye be endowed with power from on high" Luke 24:49 (KJV).

During their waiting in Jerusalem in the upper room, the Holy Spirit came upon them as a cloven tongue of fire upon the heads of each of them, and all of them started speaking in different tongues.

"And when the day of Pentecost fully came, they were all in one accord in one place. And suddenly there came a sound from heaven as of a rushing mighty wind, and it filled all the house where they were sitting. And there appeared unto them cloven tongues like as of fire, and it sat upon each of them. And they were all filled with the Holy Ghost and began to speak with other tongues as the spirit gave them utterances" Acts 2:1-4 (KJV).

At the baptism of the Holy Spirit, one is immersed or submerged in the Holy Spirit, meaning that one is under the complete control and influence of the Holy Spirit. A person who has been baptized in the Holy Spirit becomes empowered and more receptive to the influence of the Holy Spirit.

When it comes to baptism, there are different entities responsible for the different kinds of baptism:

1. The Holy Spirit is the agent who baptizes into Christ and his body.

2. The minister is the agent who baptizes with water.

3. Jesus is the agent who baptizes in the Holy Spirit.

"I indeed baptize you with water unto repentance: but he that cometh after me is mightier than I, whose shoes I am not worthy to bear: he shall baptize you with the Holy Ghost, and with fire."Matthew 3:11 (KJV). "And I knew him not: but that he should be made manifest to Israel, therefore am I come baptizing with water. And John bare record, saying, I saw the Spirit descending from heaven like a dove, and it abode upon him. And I knew him not: but he that sent me to baptize with water, the same said unto me, Upon whom thou shalt see the Spirit descending, and remaining on him, the same is he which baptizeth with the Holy Ghost." John 1:31–33 (KJV).

Chapter 4

DIFFERENT KINDS OF BAPTISM

There are 8 KINDS OF BAPTISM discussed in the bible. Each one holds unique significance and is represented through various forms and ceremonies across the breadth of biblical teachings.

Baptism of John

"John did baptize in the wilderness, and preach the baptism of repentance for the remission of sins. And there went out unto him all the land of Judaea, and they of Jerusalem, and were all baptized of him in the river of Jordan, confessing their sins." Mark 1:4-5.

"For John truly baptized with water; but ye shall be baptized with the Holy Ghost not many days hence" ... "Beginning from the baptism of John, unto that same day that he was taken up from us,

must one be ordained to be a witness with us of his resurrection"
Acts 1:5, 22.

"And he said unto them, Unto what then were ye
baptized? And they said, Unto John's baptism. Then
said Paul, John verily baptized with the baptism of
repentance, saying unto the people, that they should
believe on him which should come after him, that is,
on Christ Jesus." *Acts 19:3-4.*

More scriptural references on baptism of John: Acts 18:25, Acts
13:24, John 3:23-26, John 1:31-33, Matthew 3:1-6, Acts 10:37, and
Luke 3:3, 7, 29-30.

Christ's Baptism in Water

"After these things came Jesus and
his disciples into the land of Judaea;
and there he tarried with them, and
baptized." *John 3:22* (KJV).

"When therefore the Lord knew
how the Pharisees had heard that
Jesus made and baptized more disciples than John, (Though Jesus

himself baptized not, but his disciples)" *John 4:1-2.*

Baptism in Suffering or Cross

"But I have a baptism to be baptized with; and how am I strait-
ened till it be accomplished!" *Luke
12:50* (KJV).

*"And James and John, the sons of Zebedee, come unto him, saying,
Master, we would that thou shouldest do for us whatsoever we shall
desire. And he said unto them, What would ye that I should do for you?
They said unto him, Grant unto us that we may sit, one on thy right
hand, and the other on thy left hand, in thy glory. But Jesus said unto
them, Ye know not what ye ask: can ye drink of the cup that I drink of?
and be baptized with the baptism that I am baptized with? And they said
unto him, We can. And Jesus said unto them, Ye shall indeed drink of
the cup that I drink of; and with the baptism that I am baptized withal
shall ye be baptized." Mark 10:35-39* (KJV).

"But Jesus answered and said, Ye
know not what ye ask. Are ye able
to drink of the cup that I shall drink
of, and to be baptized with the
baptism that I am baptized with?
They say unto him, We are able.

And he saith unto them, Ye shall
drink indeed of my cup, and be
baptized with the baptism that I
am baptized with: but to sit on my
right hand, and on my left, is not
mine to give, but it shall be given
to them for whom it is prepared of
my Father." *Matthew 20:22-23.*

Baptism into Christ at Repentance and New Birth and Into His Body

"Know ye not, that so many
of us as were baptized into Jesus Christ were baptized into his
death? Therefore we are buried
with him by baptism into death:
that like as Christ was raised up
from the dead by the glory of
the Father, even so we also should
walk in newness of life." *Romans
6:3-4 (KJV).*

"Buried with him in baptism,
wherein also ye are risen with him

through the faith of the operation
of God, who hath raised him from
the dead." Colossians 2:12 (KJV).

*"For as many of you as have been baptized into Christ have put on
Christ." Galatians 3:27 (KJV).*

Baptism in the Cloud and the Sea

"Moreover, brethren, I would not
that ye should be ignorant, how
that all our fathers were under the
cloud, and all passed through the
sea; And were all baptized unto
Moses in the cloud and in the sea."
1 Corinthians 10:1-2.

Christian Baptism in Water

"Go ye therefore, and teach all nations, baptizing them in the name
of the Father, and of the Son,
and of the Holy Ghost." *Matthew
28:19.*

"He that believeth and is baptized shall be saved; but he that believeth not shall be damned." *Mark 16:16.*

Baptism in the Holy Spirit

"I indeed baptize you with water unto repentance: but he that cometh after me is mightier than I, whose shoes I am not worthy to bear: he shall baptize you with the Holy Ghost, and with fire" *Matthew 3:11* (KJV).

Baptism of Fire

"I indeed baptize you with water unto repentance. but he that cometh after me is mightier than I, whose shoes I am not worthy to bear: he shall baptize you with the Holy Ghost, and with fire." *Matthew 3:11* (KJV).

Three Baptisms for The Believer

We have three major baptisms for believers. Though other baptisms are important, especially the baptism of suffering, we will go straight into the three major baptisms that are common and essential in a believer's life.

Baptism into Christ and his body

> "For in one Spirit, we were all baptized into one body, whether Jews or Greeks, slaves or free, and we were all given one Spirit to drink" 1Corinthians: 12:13.

Regeneration is to be born again; at this point, redemption, forgiveness, deliverance, and translation into a new kingdom occur (Col 1:13). This is the meaning of being baptized into Christ and his body. Baptism into Christ enables us to have the Spirit of Jesus within us; Baptism into his body enables translation into a new kingdom to occur; the body speaks about the kingdom of God, and the body also speaks about the church of God, which is a pictorial view of the kingdom that God has destined for us. *"There is one body, and one Spirit, even as ye are called in one hope of your calling; One Lord, one faith, one baptism"* Ephesians 4:4-5 (KJV).

At this Baptism, so many things happened to us: we put on Christ, all tribes became one, access to the promises of God, and we became Abraham's seeds instead of Adamic seeds.

> "For as many of you as have been baptized into Christ have put on Christ. There is neither Jew nor Greek, there is neither bond nor free, there is neither male nor female: for ye are all one in Christ Jesus. And if

ye be Christ's, then are ye Abraham's seed, and heirs according to the promise." Galatians 3:27-29 (KJV).

The moment we realize the need for repentance and the moment we ask Jesus to come into our lives as our Lord and Saviour, automatically, this baptism takes place in our lives at the speed of light. This is more of a faith and spiritual experience, not a physical or mental experience.

Baptism of Suffering or Baptism of The Cross

"*Are they ministers of Christ? (I speak as a fool) I am more; in labours more abundant, in stripes above measure, in prisons more frequent, in deaths oft. Of the Jews five times received I forty stripes save one. Thrice was I beaten with rods, once was I stoned, thrice I suffered shipwreck, a night and a day I have been in the deep; In journeyings often, in perils of waters, in perils of robbers, in perils by mine own countrymen, in perils by the heathen, in perils in the city, in perils in the wilderness, in perils in the sea, in perils among false brethren; In weariness and painfulness, in watchings often, in hunger and thirst, in fastings often, in cold and nakedness. Beside those things that are without, that which cometh upon me daily, the care of all the churches. Who is weak, and I am not weak? who is offended, and I burn not? If I must needs glory, I will glory of the things which concern mine infirmities.*" 2 Corinthians 11:23–30 (KJV).

"And when they had laid many stripes upon them, they cast them into prison, charging the jailor to keep them safely:" Acts 16:23 (KJV).

The baptism of suffering is a mark for the kingdom of God. Only some people understand that the call to righteousness is about the pain of the cross, and every believer should understand the Baptism of suffering. It would help if you desired it, and the baptism of suffering comes with glory in return. It is something that you should undergo with happiness. Baptism into Christ is a readiness for the Baptism of suffering, whereby a believer dies to himself at the expense of others, goes hungry for others to eat, when a believer begins to fast because of the burden he has for other believers, fasts in order to remove pain from the lives of others, and personalizes the pains and burdens of others without complaining. Joy is set before any cross; the Bible says we should look unto Jesus; he endured the cross [Hebrews 12:2] to receive the prize set before him.

The baptism of suffering is an act of dying so that others may live. *"So then death worketh in us, but life in you"* 2 Corinthians 4:12 (KJV). This is a call to sacrifice, to put ourselves in a state of inconvenience for the convenience of others, to surrender the whole of ourselves to several consecrations so that others may receive the blessing of our sacrifice.

Paul began to tell us about the several afflictions he went through. This shows the sign of someone who has been baptized into the sufferings of Christ. Paul sustained so many pains for the sake of the gospel and the kingdom [2 Corinthians 11:23–28, Acts 16:23]. All the afflictions he sustained were because of the burden of the church that was laid upon him. In all the pain, he was still rejoicing; *"If I must needs glory, I will glory of the things which concern mine infirmities."* 2 Corinthians 11:30 (KJV).

Water baptism

Water baptism is done after one is saved.

> "Can anyone withhold the water to baptize these people? They have received the Holy Spirit just as we have. So, he ordered that they be baptized in the name of Jesus Christ. Then they asked him to stay for a few days" Acts 10:47-48 (KJV).

Water baptism means to be immersed in or submerged under water, and it also means to be buried in the water; during water baptism, the whole body is drowned or swallowed by water; this is a symbolic representation of the death ceremony of our partnership or participation with the death and resurrection and the newness of life we had with Jesus; it signifies that when Christ died, we died with him; when he resurrected, we resurrected with him; it shows the crucifixion of our old man; it reveals the destruction of our sinful body; so in this, we know we are no longer slaves to sin.

> "Therefore we are buried with him by baptism into death: that like as Christ was raised up from the dead by the glory of the Father, even so we also should walk in newness of life. For if we have been planted together in the likeness of his death, we shall be also in the likeness of his resurrection: Knowing this, that our old man is crucified with him, that the body of sin might be destroyed, that henceforth we should not serve sin. For he that is dead is freed from sin. Now if

we be dead with Christ, we believe that we shall also live with him: Knowing that Christ being raised from the dead dieth no more; death hath no more dominion over him" Romans 6:4–9 (KJV).

Water baptism does not remove the filth of the flesh or remit sins; rather, it is our identification with Christ in his death and resurrection. It is the physical representation of what happened to us at the new birth: the old nature dies, and a new nature replaces it. It is wrong for an unbeliever to be baptized with water. On several occasions, confession of sins was required before baptism [Mark 1:5, Mark 16:16, Acts 2:38].

Four Mysteries of Water Baptism

The act of going into the water and rising up from it demonstrates what happened to a believer at salvation. The love of God and God's redemptive nature are pictured in the work of Christ.

1. Jesus died. All died in him. *"Knowing this, that our old man is crucified with him, that the body of sin might be destroyed, that henceforth we should not serve sin. For he that is dead is freed from sin"* Romans 6:6-7 (KJV).

2. Jesus was buried. All were buried with him. *"Know ye not, that so many of us as were baptized into Jesus Christ were baptized into his death? Therefore we are buried with him by baptism into death: that like as Christ was raised up from the dead by the glory of the Father, even so we also should walk in newness of life"* Romans 6:3-4 (KJV).

3. Jesus was raised: All have a new life through his resurrection. "Therefore we are buried with him by baptism into death: that like as Christ was raised up from the dead by the glory of the Father, even so we also should walk in newness of life. For if we have been planted together in the likeness of his death, we shall be also in the likeness of his resurrection" Romans 6:4-5 (KJV).

4. Jesus ascended: All ascended, "And hath raised us up together, and made us sit together in heavenly places in Christ Jesus:" Ephesians 2:6 (KJV). "If ye then be risen with Christ, seek those things which are above, where Christ sitteth on the right hand of God" Colossians 3:1 (KJV).

Two kingdoms make up the creation of God:

1. First Adam.

2. Second Adam.

The first Adam brought all the creation under the siege of death; "For as in Adam all die, even so in Christ shall all be made alive." — 1 Corinthians 15:22.

The second Adam recreated all that was dead and made it alive in him; "But every man in his own order: Christ the firstfruits; afterward they that are Christ's at his coming." — 1 Corinthians 15:23. So, through water baptism, our burial ceremony was executed. Our resurrection to a new life was demonstrated. We declare our latest creation in Christ on the strength of this practice.

So, baptism into Christ happens before baptism in water. Baptism into Christ is baptism into death. So, when someone is baptized into Christ, a death occurs, and on the strength of that, the baptism of water is now a burial ceremony for the person who had been baptized into Christ. Water baptism symbolizes Christ's death, burial, and resurrection.

It is not essential to salvation; "*Baptism is like that. It saves you now—not because it removes dirt from your body but because it is the mark of a good conscience toward God. Your salvation comes through the resurrection of Jesus Christ.*" — 1 Peter 3:21 (CEB). Several persons were filled with the Holy Ghost without water baptism.

> "There was in the days of Herod, the king of Judaea, a certain priest named Zacharias, of the course of Abia: and his wife was of the daughters of Aaron, and her name was Elisabeth.... And it came to pass, that, when Elisabeth heard the salutation of Mary, the babe leaped in her womb; and Elisabeth was filled with the Holy Ghost:... And Mary said, My soul doth magnify the Lord, ... And his father Zacharias was filled with the Holy Ghost, and prophesied, saying," — Luke 1:5, 41, 46, 67 (KJV).

"And, behold, there was a man in Jerusalem, whose name was Simeon; and the same man was just and devout, waiting for the consolation of Israel: and the Holy Ghost was upon him. And it was revealed unto him by the Holy Ghost, that he should not see death, before he had seen the Lord's Christ. And he came by the Spirit into the temple: and when the parents brought in the child

Jesus, to do for him after the custom of the law, Then took he him up in his arms, and blessed God, and said, Lord, now lettest thou thy servant depart in peace, according to thy word: For mine eyes have seen thy salvation, Which thou hast prepared before the face of all people; A light to lighten the Gentiles, and the glory of thy people Israel. And Joseph and his mother marveled at those things which were spoken of him. And Simeon blessed them, and said unto Mary his mother, Behold, this child is set for the fall and rising again of many in Israel; and for a sign which shall be spoken against; (Yea, a sword shall pierce through thy own soul also,) that the thoughts of many hearts may be revealed. And there was one Anna, a prophetess, the daughter of Phanuel, of the tribe of Aser: she was of a great age, and had lived with an husband seven years from her virginity; And she was a widow of about fourscore and four years, which departed not from the temple, but served God with fastings and prayers night and day. And she coming in that instant gave thanks likewise unto the Lord, and spake of him to all them that looked for redemption in Jerusalem." — Luke 2:25-38 (KJV).

"Can any man forbid water, that these should not be baptized, which have received the Holy Ghost as well as we? And he commanded them to be baptized in the name of the Lord. Then prayed they him to tarry certain days" — Acts 10:47-48 (KJV).

Chapter 5

THE PURPOSE OF HOLY SPIRIT BAPTISM

There are many purposes for Holy Ghost baptism; the Spirit comes to one for a reason. When Jesus told the disciples to tarry or wait in Jerusalem for the divine Spirit, he told them the reason why they had to wait for the outpouring of the Holy Spirit, which included:

An invitation into the supernatural

"But ye shall receive power, after that the Holy Ghost is come upon you: and ye shall be witnesses unto me both in Jerusalem, and in all Judaea, and in Samaria, and unto the uttermost part of the earth." Acts 1:8

When the disciples of Jesus were baptized in the Holy Spirit, they became open to the supernatural. When one is baptized in the Holy Spirit, the Holy Spirit comes upon that person in a different dimension and with greater intensity, which activates the person's Spirit. The person's spirit is activated and opened to the supernatural or spiritual realm. When the Holy Spirit activates one's Spirit, power is imparted to the person's Spirit.

At baptism in the Holy Spirit, one's Spirit is opened to the supernatural because of the activation of the Spirit. When the spirit is activated, access is given to the supernatural. One cannot fully access the supernatural and understand the things of the Spirit.

For an effective witness

"But ye shall receive power, after that the Holy Ghost is come upon you: and ye shall be witnesses unto me both in Jerusalem, and in all Judaea, and in Samaria, and unto the uttermost part of the earth" Acts 1:8 (KJV).

The Baptism of the Holy Spirit enables us to become an effective witness of Jesus. The Holy Spirit bears witness in two ways:

1. He bears witness within us that we are God's children.

2. He bears witness to conviction in the hearts of sinners by convicting their spirits and making them aware that they need to be reconciled to God. When the Holy Spirit came upon the disciples at Jerusalem, the first miracle he used them to do was to bear witness, and at the end of the witness, 3,000 souls were added to the kingdom of God. For an effective witness to be done, one needs the baptism of the Holy Spirit, because it is the Holy Spirit that enables us to bear witness. God wants men to be reconciled to him, and Jesus Christ himself told us to go into the world and make disciples of all nations, but all of these things cannot be achieved without the power that comes through the

baptism of the Holy Spirit.

For Effective Prayer Life

The enterprise of prayer cannot be achieved without the help of the Holy Spirit because it is the Spirit himself that helps us to pray, as a result of the fall of man. We are laden with many infirmities, but the Holy Spirit helps our infirmities by giving us the utterance of prayer. We cannot effectively pray for the mind of God without the help of the Holy Spirit, because we don't know the mind of God, for no man knows the mind of God except the Spirit of God.

> "But God hath revealed them unto us by his Spirit: for the Spirit searcheth all things, yea, the deep things of God" 1 Corinthians 2:10 (KJV).

The Holy Spirit helps us to pray by searching the mind of God and giving us the utterance to pray about it; we cannot pray on our own without the help of the Holy Spirit. Additionally, the Spirit facilitates our ability to pray by providing us with the burdens or needs for prayer; the burdens and desires for prayer ultimately lead us to the prayer closet. Thus, the Spirit also assists us in praying more effectively by providing these things for us. We cannot pray consistently without an urge to pray, which the Holy Spirit bestows upon us.

For Unity-Oneness-Togetherness

"For by one Spirit are we all baptized into one body, whether we be Jews or Gentiles, whether we be bond or free; and have been all made to drink into one Spirit." 1 Corinthians 12:13

The Holy Spirit helps or enables us to be united as one body; the Baptism of the Holy Spirit came upon the believers when they were united in the upper room [Acts 2:1]. One of the signs of the Holy Spirit is peace and unity. The Holy Spirit came to bring unity to the lives of believers in two areas.

Unity with God.

Unity with God is the initial oneness the Holy Spirit establishes between us. Reconciliation is the term used to describe this kind of oneness. The Holy Spirit brings us closer to God during the reconciliation process. Man was estranged from God due to sin in the Garden of Eden; however, the Holy Spirit makes amends our relationship with God and unites us.

Unity With Our Fellow Human Being.

The Holy Spirit helps us to be in unity with our fellow human beings by allowing us to tolerate and endure one another. The Holy Spirit also achieves this in us by giving us love; in Romans 5:5"*And hope maketh not ashamed; because the love of God is shed abroad in our hearts by the Holy Ghost which is given unto us.*" The Holy Spirit sheds his love on our hearts while also imparting the ability to love one another. The main thing that the devil fights in the body of Christ is unity or oneness because, whenever there is no unity, the Holy Spirit cannot establish unity. Oneness is one of the main features of the presence of the Holy Spirit in the life of a believer. Jesus intensely prayed for unity among his disciples ["*That they all may be one; as thou, Father, art in me, and I in thee, that they also may be one in us: that the world may believe that thou hast sent me.*" - John 17:21], and this was achieved ["*And when they heard that, they lifted up their voice to God with one accord, and said, Lord, thou art God, which hast made heaven, and earth, and the sea, and all that in them is.*" - Acts 4:24]. The disciples are always in one accord, making it easy for the Holy Spirit to flow among them.

For Identification

"Wherefore tongues are for a sign, not to them that believe, but to them that believe not: but prophesying serveth not for them that believe not, but for them which believe." 1 Corinthians 14:22 (KJV).

The Baptism of the Holy Spirit with the evidence of praying in tongues is one of the ways of identification showing that we are God's children, especially to unbelievers, because it is a supernatural ability that is only given to believers at the Baptism of the Holy Spirit. Also, at the Baptism of the Holy Spirit, the spiritual abilities of God that are deposited in our Spirit are activated. The functionality of those abilities within us contributes to our identity as God's children.

Signs and wonders were given to the apostles of Jesus Christ, confirming their status as God's children. "*And by the hands of the apostles were many signs and wonders wrought among the people; (and they were all with one accord in Solomon's porch. And of the rest durst no man join himself to them: but the people magnified them. And believers were the more added to the Lord, multitudes both of men and women)*" Acts 5:12–14.

At the Baptism of the Holy Spirit, our Spirit is brought into the full measure of the Holy Spirit, which goes a long way toward patterning our lives differently. This includes a change of ideology, mindset, dressing, mode of conduct, talking, and character. The character change helps identify us as children of God. "*And when he had found him, he brought him unto Antioch. And it came to pass, that a whole year they assembled themselves with the church, and taught much people. And the disciples were called Christians first in Antioch*" Acts 11:26. The disciples were identified as Christians because of how their lives were patterned after the Holy Spirit baptized them.

Chapter 6

MISCONCEPTIONS OF PEOPLE ABOUT BAPTISM

Is the Holy Spirit's baptism for everyone?

The Holy Spirit baptism is for all who believe. The holy spirit baptism is a promise that God gave his people that on the last day, he would pour out his Spirit on all flesh.

"And it shall come to pass in the last days, saith God, I will pour out of my Spirit upon all flesh: and your sons and your daughters shall prophesy, and your young men shall see visions, and your old men shall dream dreams: And on my servants and on my handmaidens I will pour out in those days of my Spirit; and they shall prophesy: And I will shew wonders in heaven above, and signs in the earth beneath; blood, and fire, and vapour of smoke." Acts 2:17–19

A person who accepts Jesus Christ as their Saviour can receive the Holy Spirit's baptism. The presence of Jesus in the life of a believer ushers him into the baptism of the Holy Spirit.

Is Holy Ghost baptism a criterion for making heaven?

Holy Spirit baptism is not a criterion for making heaven; however, Holy Spirit baptism empowers us to effectively live for God on earth. *"Jesus answered and said unto him, Verily, verily, I say unto thee, Except a man be born again, he cannot see the kingdom of God"* John 3:3. The only criterion for making heaven is to be born again. But when a person is born again without the Baptism [outpouring of the Holy Spirit upon his life], such an individual cannot fully enjoy the provision of the things that were freely given to him at the new birth.

> "For to be carnally minded is death; but to be spiritually minded is life and peace." Romans 8:6. "But the natural man receiveth not the things of the Spirit of God: for they are foolishness unto him: neither can he know them, because they are spiritually discerned." 1 Corinthians 2:14 (KJV).

The spiritual life is based on the Spirit. We must be spiritual to receive things from God, and our spiritual senses can also be activated. Without our baptism in him, the Spirit of God cannot lead us to great lengths, and one of the proofs that shows that we are children of God is to be led by the Holy Spirit (Romans 8:14).

Must I be baptized in the Holy Spirit?

For a believer to effectively walk in the Spirit and have a victorious Christian life, such a believer must be baptized in the Spirit. Baptism of the Holy Spirit is not a must, but for a believer to experience a deeper dimension in the spirit, they must be baptized in the Holy Spirit, and God cannot use us deep in the supernatural if we are not baptized in the Holy Spirit. The Christian journey becomes clear to us when we are baptized in the Holy Spirit and begin to understand who we are as Christians entirely. The disciples of Jesus couldn't bear and understand some of the teachings of Jesus until they were baptized in the Holy Spirit. "*I have yet many things to say unto you, but ye cannot bear them now. Howbeit when he, the Spirit of truth, is come, he will guide you into all truth: for he shall not speak of himself; but whatsoever he shall hear, that shall he speak: and he will shew you things to come*" John 16:12–13.

After the Baptism of the Holy Spirit in the disciples' lives, they began to understand and bear all that Jesus had told them. So, a believer needs to be baptized in the Holy Spirit.

Is the Holy Ghost Baptism a promise?

The Holy Ghost baptism is a promise from God to all believers.

> "For the promise is unto you, and to your children, and to all that are afar off, even as many as the Lord our God shall call" Acts 2:39 (KJV).

God promised the Israelites through the mouth of prophet Joel that he would pour out his Spirit on all flesh [Joel 2:28], which means that everyone, no matter their position, is qualified to receive the full measure and outpouring of the Holy Spirit and to come under his influence. God told them that the time to fulfill the promise is on the latter or last day. The promise was fulfilled on the day of Pentecost when God poured out his Spirit on the disciples in the upper room, and the disciples were neither priests nor prophets nor kings but people of different professions and occupations, including women.

Is Holy Ghost baptism a sign of being born again?

Being born again is demonstrated by the fruit we yield, not by receiving the Holy Spirit baptism.

> "Even so every good tree bringeth forth good fruit; but a corrupt tree bringeth forth evil fruit. A good tree cannot bring forth evil fruit, neither can a corrupt tree bring forth good fruit. Every tree that bringeth not forth good fruit is hewn down, and cast into the fire. Wherefore by their fruits ye shall know them. Not every one that saith unto me, Lord, Lord, shall enter into the kingdom of heaven; but he that doeth the will of my Father which is in heaven" Matthew 7:17–21 (KJV).

People cannot see if a person is born again since it is an internal work of God in our Spirit; instead, they can only determine if we are truly born again by the fruits of our lifestyle. It is easier for a Christian who is baptized in the Holy Spirit to bear much fruit for God than one who is not, and the fruits are listed in [Gal 3:22–23]. Nevertheless, baptism in the Holy Spirit helps us to bear fruit [live right] even in challenging situations [hard times]. These fruits serve as an indication that we are new creations.

Is all worthy for Baptism of the Holy Spirit?

All are not worthy of the Baptism of the Holy Spirit; the only set of people deserving of the Baptism of the Holy Spirit are those who have repented of their sins. "*Then Peter said unto them, Repent, and be baptized every one of you in the name of Jesus Christ for the remission of sins, and ye shall receive the gift of the Holy Ghost*" Acts 2:38. The presence of Jesus through repentance makes an individual worthy of being baptized by the Holy Spirit. Nobody can be baptized with the Holy Spirit outside of Jesus. It is he whom John the Baptist said that he will baptize with the holy Spirit and with fire. "*I indeed baptize you with water unto repentance. But he that cometh after me is mightier than I, whose shoes I am not worthy to bear: he shall baptize you with the Holy Ghost, and with fire*" Matthew 3:11.

All are not worthy to be baptized, only those that the holy Spirit sanctifies. "*That I should be the minister of Jesus Christ to the Gentiles, ministering the gospel of God, that the offering up of the Gentiles might be acceptable, being sanctified by the Holy Ghost*" Romans 15:16. Through the sanctification that comes from the holy Spirit, we are made acceptable and worthy to be baptized by the same Spirit.

Who can baptize me with the Holy Spirit?

Any spirit-filled believer can baptize any believer who is willing with the holy Spirit; it is through human vessels that God uses to get his own baptized with the holy Spirit.

> "While Peter yet spake these words, the Holy Ghost fell on all them which heard the word. And they of the circumcision which believed were astonished, as many as came with Peter, because that on the Gentiles also was poured out the gift of the Holy Ghost. For they heard them speak with tongues, and magnify God. Then answered Peter, Can any man forbid water, that these should not be baptized, which have received the Holy Ghost as well as we?" Acts 10:44–47 (KJV).

While Peter was talking to Cornelius, God used him to get Cornelius and his household baptized with the Holy Spirit. "*And when Paul had laid his hands upon them, the Holy Ghost came on them; and they spake with tongues, and prophesied*" Acts 19:6]. Here, God used Paul to baptize twelve men with the Holy Ghost. Any human vessel that has been baptized with the Holy Ghost and is full of faith can be used by God to get others baptized in the holy ghost, regardless of the person's gender, tribe, race, color, etc., provided the vessel is available and usable by God. God can use the vessel to get others baptized with the holy ghost.

What are the conditions for the baptism of the Holy Spirit?

The condition for the baptism of the Holy Spirit is repentance [Acts 2:33]. Repentance prepares the spirit of man to receive the outpour of the Holy Spirit [Mark 2:21–22]. Our old human sinful nature cannot accommodate the Holy Spirit; the power of the Holy Spirit will tear it down. Only a renewed, regenerated spirit can accommodate the outpouring of the Holy Spirit; that is why Jesus said that you could not put new wine in an old wineskin because the old wineskin cannot accommodate it. Moreover, another condition for the Baptism of the Holy Spirit is believing in the Holy Spirit, and that is by believing that the Holy Spirit is given to everyone and can be received by everyone who desires him. People have many wrong beliefs about the Baptism of the Holy Spirit, and these beliefs go a long way in hindering them from being baptized in the Holy Spirit. For one to be baptized in the Holy Spirit, one has to believe in the Holy Spirit and also in the Baptism of the Holy Spirit.

However, another essential condition for the Baptism of the Holy Spirit is desire; our desire for the Holy Spirit draws him to us. "*In the last day, that great day of the feast, Jesus stood and cried, saying, If any man thirst, let him come unto me, and drink. He that believeth on me, as the scripture hath said, out of his belly shall flow rivers of living water.*" — John 7:37-38 KJV.

Baptism of the Holy Ghost is easy when we desire it; God said every thirsty heart should be filled.

"For he satisfieth the longing soul,
and filleth the hungry soul with
goodness." — Psalm 107:9 KJV.

Our hunger for the Holy Spirit makes us seek after him, and when we seek after him, he comes to baptize us with his presence. God promised to sanctify our hunger whenever we are hungry after him. Through our desire and hunger, petitions are made unto God, and God grants an answer to our petition by sending his Spirit to baptize us.

"If ye then, being evil, know how to give good gifts unto your children: how much more shall your heavenly Father give the Holy Spirit to them that ask him?" — Luke 11:13 KJV.

Must you fall under the power to receive the baptism of the Holy Spirit?

You must not fall under power to receive. When Paul was baptized with the Holy Spirit, he did not fall under power but was filled with the Holy Spirit. Receiving the Holy Spirit is a matter of faith; we receive him by faith. Falling under power is a physical manifestation of what we have already received. The most important thing is to be filled with the Holy Spirit, whether we fall under its power or not. It depends on how the Holy Spirit chooses to manifest himself in the life of a believer.

Chapter 7

HINDRANCES TO THE BAPTISM OF THE HOLY SPIRIT

There are major hindrances to the baptism of the Holy Spirit which are classified into personal hindrances and general hindrances.

Personal hindrances

Personal hindrances are individual hindrances or factors that can cause impediments to the Baptism of the Holy Spirit; these are conditions of the heart, like ideologies, misconceptions, and the wrong state of understanding the secret things of the kingdom.

Ignorance

The word of God expressly said in 1 Corinthians 12:1, "Now concerning spiritual gifts, brethren, I would not have you ignorant." The word ignorance in the kingdom is darkness; lack of revelation is an absence of light to a believer. A believer who lacks knowledge and understanding is like someone in the dark room without light for sight. If you are not informed, you will be deformed. The Apostle Paul met some Christians in Ephesus who were not baptized in the Holy Spirit because they didn't know that there was such an experience. That is why it is better to be taught for an adequate baptism, because:

1. Some are not aware.

2. Some have not heard about Holy Ghost baptism.

3. Some have heard but don't know how to receive.

4. Some have heard but don't know that it is a gift to all that are saved.

"And there appeared unto them cloven tongues like as of fire, and it sat upon each of them. And they were all filled with the Holy Ghost, and began to speak with other tongues, as the Spirit gave them utterance. And there were dwelling at Jerusalem Jews, devout men, out of every nation under heaven. Now when this was noised abroad, the multitude came together, and were confounded, because that every man heard them speak in his own language. And they were all amazed and marvelled, saying one to another, Behold, are not all these which speak Galilaeans? And how hear we every man in our own tongue, wherein we were born? Parthians, and Medes, and Elamites, and the dwellers in Mesopotamia, and in Judaea, and Cappadocia, in Pontus, and Asia." Acts 2:3–9 (KJV).

Fear

Some are afraid because they have not had that experience before. Several times when I have a meeting like the outpouring of the Holy Spirit, I have noticed something common in the lives of some individuals: they are afraid of speaking in tongues because they don't want to say something wrong that will grieve the Holy Spirit, and as a result of that, they can quench the Holy Spirit some times.

1. Fear of acting abnormally; Acts 2:13–14: "*Others mocking said, These men are full of new wine. But Peter, standing up with the eleven, lifted up his voice, and said unto them, Ye men of Judaea, and all ye that dwell at Jerusalem, be this known unto you, and hearken to my words:*"

2. Fear of condemnation and judgment from God because of their past lives.

3. Fear of receiving the wrong spirit.

4. Some are also afraid of falling under the power of God.

5. Feelings and misconceptions.

Baptism of the Spirit is not feeling-based but faith-based; it is a spiritual experience, not a physical experience. Some think that to be baptized in the Spirit, you must have a definite experience. When it comes to individual experiences during Baptism, the Spirit of God chooses how he manifests through the individual; there are some that shout and move mightily under the power, while some are very calm as a gentle breeze, yet they are blasting in tongues, and some fall under power while some stand or even sit. Some people sometimes become conscious, while others are so much unconscious. The Spirit moves through us as he wills.

> "But all these worketh that one and the selfsame Spirit, dividing to every man severally as he will." — 1 Corinthians 12:11 KJV.

Feelings and misconceptions are vital hindrances

1. Some believers feel that they are not worthy.

2. Some feel that, due to the background they came from, they cannot receive the Holy Spirit.

3. Some believe that baptism in the Holy Spirit is only for those that are called into ministry. The word of God clearly clarifies this in Acts 2:38–39: *"Then Peter said unto them, Repent, and be baptized every one of you in the name of Jesus Christ for the remission of sins, and ye shall receive the gift of the Holy Ghost. For the promise is unto you, and to your children, and to all that are afar off, even as many as the Lord our God shall call."*

4. Some think it is an individual gift, only for some not for everybody.

5. Some depend on signs to be convinced that they have received the Holy Spirit.

6. Some think they need to tarry before they can be baptized.

7. Some think they need to be believers for a long time before they can receive Holy Ghost baptism.

8. Some think they need to grow into spiritual capacity and experience before receiving the Holy Ghost's baptism.

I had a believer who told me that he could not speak in tongues because God did not give it to him and that it was not the will of God for him. He even told me that the Bible says in 1 Corinthians 12:10, "*to another the working of miracles, to another prophecy, to another discerning of spirits, to other divers' kinds of tongues, to another the interpretation of tongues.*" He was trying to make the point that tongues were only given to specific individuals, and he wasn't in the category of people who were to receive the spirit with evidence of speaking in tongues. The promise made to all believers in Mark 16:16 is that everyone who believes will experience the baptism of the Holy Spirit and with the evidence of speaking in tongues.

"He that believeth and is baptized shall be saved; but he that believeth not shall be damned" Mark 16:16 (KJV).

Wrong teaching

Knowledge has destroyed many people. Teaching shapes people. It is possible that a generation can be wrong, and it is likely that a congregation of 1,000 can be wrong while one among them can be right. Knowledge is power; knowledge is essential; knowledge is authority. The authority of a believer is easily exercised on the strength of knowledge. When it comes to the kingdom of God, any area in the kingdom you are ignorant of is the area of your undoing; it's the area of your impediment, and it is the area of your limitation. Some believers have been limited from receiving the Holy Spirit because of wrong teachings that they have been equipped with.

There are some definite wrong doctrines that some believers have:

1. Some believe that it is wrong to receive the Holy Spirit's baptism.

2. Others think that the Holy Spirit stopped coming upon people after the Apostles.

3. Some think there is a price tag, so based on that, they think you must fast and pray before you can receive the baptism.

4. Some think that it is only given to some.

Unwillingness

Showing an unwilling attitude, which is a lack of desire and being reluctant towards the Holy Spirit, goes a long way toward hindering someone from being baptized with the Holy Spirit. The Holy Spirit doesn't force Himself on people. To be baptized with him, the person must be willing to do so. It is our willingness towards him that get us baptized with him; when he sees that we desire to be baptized with him, he comes to us and fulfills our desire. Many people are not baptized with the Holy Spirit because they are unwilling.

Lack of interest

Lack of concern and attention towards Holy Ghost baptism can withdraw the Holy Spirit from filling us up with him, when one is not concerned about the Holy Ghost. It limits the operations of the Spirit within and around him. When we pay attention to the Holy Spirit, he makes us focus on him and comes to fill us. The Holy Spirit loves it when people are focused on him, because focus shows that we are interested in him [Lk 11:13]. The Holy Spirit does not hesitate to fill those who are focused on him. So, a lack of focus and interest limits us from getting baptized with the Holy Spirit.

Heart conditions:

The heart of a believer is the most prominent place of transaction in the whole world; the word of God advises us to keep our heart with all diligence, for out of it are the issues of life. Life matters deny us focus and concentration, and the Holy Spirit cannot flow where there is disorder. Imagine baptizing someone with a lousy heart condition in the Holy Spirit; it will be very difficult, unless, by the mercy of God. A heart condition such as an internal distraction that has to do with funds, family burden, broken home, wrong knowledge and gossip about the church, baptizing individuals with such heart conditions in the Spirit can hinder the baptism of the Holy Spirit.

"Keep thy heart with all diligence; for out of it are the issues of life." — Proverbs 4:23 KJV.

Lack of concentration

The Holy Spirit is a person; you can grieve him, quench him, and resist him. We have so many factors that can lead to a lack of concentration, and there are two kinds of distraction we usually see in the life of the believer, which is

1. Internal distraction and

2. External distraction

We have mentioned internal distractions in heart conditions, but I will focus on external distractions, like cell phones. Focusing on people's facial expressions during prayers can distract you. Until you reach a point of maximum focus on the Spirit; if not, it can be a very big hindrance.

Unbelief or doubt

The greatest limitation or weapon that hinders the movement of the Spirit is unbelief. In Matthew 13:58, Jesus could not do mighty works because of their unbelief. Secondly, in another account in Heb. 3:19, the children of God could not enter into the rest of God because of their unbelief. There is nothing impossible for anyone who has faith (Matthew 17:20).

Unbelief or doubt is hazardous, like a thorn that kills any seed of the word that a believer receives. I have come in contact with some believers who are filled with unbelievers, and I have tried so much to Baptize them in the Holy Spirit, still it is as though I poured water into a sieve. But the moment I spot the individual, I automatically fix them on Bible studies and meditation, and the moment that doubt clears, the Spirit of God takes hold of them. The word of God is the key that flushes and clears doubt and unbelief, and also the convicting power of the Holy Spirit.

Lack of appetite and hunger for God

Lack of appetite can cause the presence of God to be withdrawn from a believer; what ignites the presence of God in a believer is an appetite for righteousness and more of him; nothing speeds up the presence of the Holy Spirit more like hunger. Hunger for God proves that you long for him; there is a prophetic word for this, throughout the scripture, people who were hungry for God are filled, and there is an open check-in [Jn 7:37–38]. If you are thirsty, you will be filled. Some percentage of believers in our generation today have a hunger that the Holy Spirit birthed. In [Acts 9:1–9] Paul's encounter came by sovereignty; the same account happened in the acts of the Apostle, a certain woman named Lydia; God opened her heart and birthed hunger in her on the strength of that she was able to give attention to the apostles [Acts 16:14]. Sometimes, while getting believers filled with the Holy Spirit, we struggle to get believers who lack spiritual hunger filled with the Holy Spirit.

There are a lot of things that can ignite hunger and an appetite for God.

1. The word of God.

The word of God contained testimonies of realities that can ignite a compelling force and an incredible desire for the knowledge of God.

2. Intercession.

When the ministry of intercession is exercised on behalf of a soul, or maybe when participatory prayer is going on over a soul, suddenly, something about the person begins to change [Lk 2:8].

3. Holy Spirit.

Through God's love, the Spirit of Jesus is lavishly release upon individuals, on the strength of that he begins to do internal work in their lives. The Spirit always births hunger in the life of a believer. [Jn 6:63]

4. Association.

Several times, I have seen people who have zero appetite for God suddenly pick up and emerge because of followership and friendship, particularly when they observe their friends—whom they are aware are sinners—turn to holiness, experience the gift of the Holy Spirit, and manifest speaking in tongues. This inspires a deep longing for the Holy Spirit, sparking holy fear and an incredible desire for the outpouring of the Holy Spirit.

5. Testimonies of others.

In Luke, Jesus ordered a man he delivered to go home and testify for his freedom; Jesus knew the purpose of testimony. Testimony has a way of uplifting individuals who have previously placed their belief in God, giving others hope that they can receive from heaven, inspiring others, and preparing the heart for a genuine encounter [Lk 8:38–39].

Foundation

The foundation of the believer is vital, and it has a role to play when it comes to baptism; the word foundation prepares a child of God for effective baptism. When it comes to foundation, we also have individuals from different family backgrounds. We have people who are under the siege of the contracted spirit and others who are under the blockade of the contacted spirit.

Contracted spirit is a result of legal family covenants that were initiated in a family as a result of ignorance or transgenerational covenants that were passed over to the family. While contracted Spirit results from an individual's wrong lifestyle, either by association, by mirroring the lives of others, or by making the wrong person a role model.

All these are dealt with at the salvational level, but when they are not dealt with, it will result to hindrances, remember it is salvation before baptism, don't force yourself to baptize someone who is not saved in the Holy Spirit. I have seen where sometimes we have to minister deliverance to a believer before we can get them baptized in the Spirit; ministering baptism to believers that have the presence of an unclean spirit can cause a hindrance, unclean spirits those not have access to the spirit of a believer but can influence its body as a result of wrong life style. On several occasions, we have to remind them of what Jesus did on the cross: on the strength of the revelation of the cross, you break the chains of darkness and stronghold over their lives.

"Who hath delivered us from the power of darkness, and hath translated us into the kingdom of his dear Son."Colossians 1:13 (KJV).

General Hindrances

Weak believer or weak priest

Sometimes, in this aspect, the believer to be baptized is ready. Prepared by the word of God, but the believer who is to be the instrument for the baptism is weak due to sin, pride, wrong motive, and wrong state of heart; it can hinder the baptism with the Holy Spirit.

Environment

During Jesus' earthly ministry, He considered environment a factor; God is everywhere but does not manifest everywhere. Sometimes, we go to the mountains or different prayer camps, not because God is not with us or within our homes, but because we choose to move out to a conducive environment to avoid distractions. The movement of the Spirit is always within us, but a conducive environment allows us to become sensitive to the Spirit within us (Lk 24:49).

Atmosphere

It is crucial to consider the atmosphere regarding the Baptism in the Spirit and the law of spiritual habitation. Atmosphere speaks about the condition of an environment; it speaks about ambiance; it could be aura. The atmosphere can sometimes determine the operations of a spirit in a territory.

> "And when the day of Pentecost was fully come, they were all with one accord in one place. And suddenly there came a sound from heaven as of a rushing mighty wind, and it filled all the house where they were sitting" — Acts 2:1-2 KJV.

Two Kinds of Atmosphere

Cooperate or congregational atmosphere

When enough worship is generated in the service or intercession of the saints has risen to the point that everyone in the meeting is gazing toward heaven. No wonder the Bible says not to neglect the gathering of the brethren. People can quickly be baptized in the Spirit in such an atmosphere [Psalm 113].

Individual or personal atmosphere

This has to do with the personal altar of a believer; when you have so much given yourself to the secret place of prayer, at that point, you create a strong spiritual atmosphere, and the easiest way to do this, is by becoming a worshipper. Worship alters an existing atmosphere and creates an atmosphere for the presence of the Holy Spirit. We are custodians of different atmospheres, and when we go deep into the dimensions of atmosphere, we will find out that they are in their various categories; there are people with dynamic and more profound atmospheres, and when they appear, they don't need prayers for things to happen; just at their appearance, several things will begin to happen. the atmosphere you generate from your altar can become solvency anywhere you appear. When you don't understand that the degree which you flow with the spirit of God is a product of the secret place it can cause impediments or hindrances to the baptize people in the Holy Spirit. To easily fill people with the Holy Spirit, you must have an excellent spiritual atmosphere; getting people filled with the Holy Spirit does not only happen in the church. People can get filled and be baptized in the Spirit anytime, anywhere, and at any moment.

Chapter 8

INDIVIDUAL EVIDENCE OF HOLY GHOST BAPTISM

The main evidence of Holy Spirit baptism throughout scripture is speaking in tongues, as vividly demonstrated on the Day of Pentecost.

> "And they were all filled with the Holy Ghost, and began to speak with other tongues, as the Spirit gave them utterance" Acts 2:4 (KJV).

The first time the Holy Spirit was poured out upon believers on earth, the most distinct evidence was that each spoke in other tongues.

When Peter visited the household of Cornelius, he witnessed this evidence firsthand. While he shared the Gospel, the Holy Spirit descended upon all who heard the word.

> "While Peter yet spake these words, the Holy Ghost fell on all them which heard the word. And they of the circumcision which believed were astonished, as many as came with Peter, because that on the Gentiles also

was poured out the gift of the Holy Ghost. For they heard them speak with tongues, and magnify God." Acts 10:44-46 (KJV).

Similarly, in Ephesus, Paul encountered twelve men who were followers of Christ but had not yet received the Holy Spirit. After Paul explained the full gospel to them, he laid his hands on them, and they began to speak in new tongues.

"And when Paul had laid his hands upon them, the Holy Ghost came on them; and they spake with tongues, and prophesied" Acts 19:6 (KJV).

Jesus Christ himself declared that speaking in tongues would be one of the signs that follow believers.

"And these signs shall follow them that believe; In my name shall they cast out devils; they shall speak with new tongues;" Mark 16:17 (KJV).

Many have argued that speaking in tongues is not the main evidence of Holy Ghost baptism and that it's not a must that all believers who are filled with the Holy Spirit speak in tongues, but looking into the scriptures, one will find out that the first evidence that shows that one has been baptized with the Holy Spirit is speaking in tongues.

Some go to the extent of arguing whether Paul spoke in tongues when he was baptized with the Holy Ghost. Here, the Apostle

Paul's own experience adds depth to this discussion. He explicitly expressed gratitude for his ability to speak in tongues more than anyone else in the Corinthian church.

"I thank my God, I speak with tongues more than ye all" 1 Corinthians 14:18 (KJV).

Some believers do not speak in tongues immediately following their baptism in the Holy Spirit, many find themselves doing so spontaneously later, often during prayer. While some get surprised when they find out that they are praying in a language or manner that is strange to them. The tongues are evidence that shows that something has taken place within them.

It is important to acknowledge that while speaking in tongues is a significant and common evidence of the Holy Spirit's baptism, it is part of a broader spectrum of spiritual gifts bestowed upon believers for the edification of the church and the furtherance of the Gospel. As believers grow in faith and spiritual maturity, they may experience various gifts as the Holy Spirit wills, each serving a unique and divine purpose within the body of Christ.

Chapter 9

SCRIPTURAL EVIDENCE FOR THE BAPTISM OF THE HOLYSPIRIT

These are the evidence or proof that so many people in the Bible received the Holy Spirit. The Bible says that every word may be established in the mouth of two or three witnesses. *"But if he will not listen, take one or two others along, so that 'every matter may be established by the testimony of two or three witnesses"* Matthew 18:16.

On the day of Pentecost, the apostles were baptized.

"And when the day of Pentecost was fully come, they were all with one accord in one place. And suddenly there came a sound from heaven as of a rushing mighty wind, and it filled all the house where they were sitting. And there appeared unto them cloven tongues like as of fire, and it sat upon each of them. And they were all filled with the Holy Ghost, and began to speak with other tongues, as the Spirit gave them utterance." Acts 2:1-4 (KJV).

Everyone in the upper room spoke in tongues to a level that drew the attention of unbelievers.

Believers at Samaria

> "Now when the apostles which were at Jerusalem heard that Samaria had received the word of God, they sent unto them Peter and John: Who, when they were come down, prayed for them, that they might receive the Holy Ghost: (For as yet he was fallen upon none of them: only they were baptized in the name of the Lord Jesus.) Then laid they their hands on them, and they received the Holy Ghost." Acts 8:14-17 (KJV).

With the help of the Holy Ghost, I understood that the Holy Ghost cannot be received by offering money. A certain man in the scriptures named Simon saw that through the laying on of the apostle's hands, the Holy Ghost was given; he offered them money [Acts 8:18]. We have discussed the criteria in this book, which will guide you on an excellent way to receive the Holy Spirit. If you read the previous verse, Acts 8:5, the Bible says that Philip preached to them, they heard the word of God, an internal work of the Spirit was done in their lives before the outpouring, Peter and John did not lay hands on them until they heard that they had received Jesus as their personal Lord and saviour [Acts 8:14]. On several occasions, I asked someone, "Have you received the baptism in the Holy Spirit with evidence of speaking in tongues?" The individual responded and said that their pastor does not speak in tongues. Which means it is not a valid truth, that your pastor does not believe in speaking in other tongues is not a limitation to you; the infilling of the Spirit is an individual journey. It is a revelational journey; the day you come to light will be when a change occurs.

Paul's encounter with Ananias:

> "So, Ananias went to the house, and when he arrived, he placed his hands on Saul. "Brother Saul," he said, "the Lord Jesus, who appeared to you on the road as you were coming here, has sent me so that you may see again and be filled with the Holy Spirit." Acts 9:17 (KJV).

After Paul met Jesus in Acts 9:5, an ordination was birthed in the life of Paul in Acts 9:15. Paul's encounter was by God's grace, a result of God's sovereignty. There have been several occasions where the baptism of the Spirit happened through divine intervention.

Cornelius and his household:

> "While Peter yet spake these words, the Holy Ghost fell on all them which heard the word. And they of the circumcision which believed were astonished, as many as came with Peter, because that on the Gentiles also was poured out the gift of the Holy Ghost. For they heard them speak with tongues, and magnify God." Acts 10:44-46 (KJV).

The hunger and thirst in Cornelius was so massive that it led him to fast; his hunger engineered the mercy of God in his entire household.

> "And Cornelius said, Four days ago I was fasting until this hour; and at the ninth hour I prayed in my house, and, behold, a man stood before me in bright clothing, And said, Cornelius, thy prayer is heard, and thine alms are had in remembrance in the sight of God." Acts 10:30-31 (KJV).

The disciples in Ephesus:

"While Apollos was at Corinth, Paul passed through the interior and came to Ephesus. There, he found some disciples, and asked them, "Did you receive the Holy Spirit when you became believers?" "No," they answered, "we have not even heard that there is a Holy Spirit. Into what, then, were you baptized?" Paul asked. "The baptism of John," they replied; Paul explained: John's baptism was a baptism of repentance. He told the people to believe in the One coming after him, that is, in Jesus. On hearing this, they were baptized in the name of the Lord Jesus. And when Paul laid his hands on them, the Holy Spirit came upon them, and they spoke in tongues and prophesied. There were about twelve men in all" Acts 19:1-7 (KJV).

The believers at Ephesus have not received the Holy Ghost because of ignorance. In Acts 19:2, Paul asked them, but they don't know much about the Baptism in the Holy Spirit; there are so many believers in that condition that have not heard about the Baptism of the Holy Spirit, and as a result of their lack of awareness, it prevented them from being baptized. There is nothing that prevents the Baptism of the Holy Spirit like ignorance. It is ignorance that has prevented individuals from speaking in tongues numerous times. A significant portion of Christians have experienced this, and some have even been informed of it; nevertheless, due to incorrect teaching and a narrow religious perspective, it has become a barrier for them.

Chapter 10

FACTORS FOR EFFECTIVE BAPTISM

Born again

Repentance is the first step in receiving the baptism of the Holy Spirit. Apostle Peter made it clear in Acts 2:38: repent and be baptized, and you may receive the gift of the Holy Spirit.

> "Peter replied, "Repent and be baptized, every one of you, in the name of Jesus Christ for the forgiveness of your sins, and you will receive the gift of the Holy Spirit" Acts: 2:38 (KJV).

Remember, he said the 'gift' of the Holy Spirit, not the 'gifts' of the Holy Spirit'. The Gift of the Holy Spirit speaks about the person of the Holy Spirit. The Gifts of the Holy Spirit speak about the charismatic abilities that come from the person of the Holy Spirit.

> "Now there are diversities of gifts, but the same Spirit. ... But all these worketh that one and the selfsame Spirit, dividing to every man severally as he will." 1 Corinthians 12:4-11 (KJV).

Desire

> "On the last and greatest day of the feast, Jesus stood up
> and called out in a loud voice, "If anyone is thirsty, let
> him come to Me and drink" John: 7:37 (KJV).

Desires give birth to an unquenchable taste and appetite for God. The Bible says in Matthew 5:6 that the thirsty shall be filled. Out of desires David was able to long for God in Psalms 42, 73, and 132. An individual with desire always attracts the presence of God. In some of my programs, when I see people with desire, the moment I pray for them, they easily get baptized in the Spirit.

Knowledge

> "My people are destroyed by a lack of knowledge.
> Because you have rejected knowledge, I will also reject
> you as one of my priests. Since you have forgotten
> the law of your God, I will also forget your children"
> Hosea. 4:6 (KJV).

The ability to understand the person of the Holy Spirit is knowledge; not knowing is your undoing in the kingdom; any area of the supernatural you are ignorant of is the area of your limitation, but any area that you adequately understand with knowledge is the area of your manifestation. Everything about the kingdom of

God is encoded in revelation, and revelation comes through the knowledge of the word of God. When you don't know that the things of the Spirit are freely given to you, you will never walk in them. I have often seen believers being hindered from definite manifestations and spiritual experiences because they don't know about them. Many dimensions of the Spirit have been questioned because many do not know, and when they fail to realize it, they fight to question some operations of the Spirit. It's essential to know, but irrespective of whether there is a role for knowledge, the mercy of God supersedes knowledge; for even knowing is access; by the love of God, he can still grant you access. The Bible says in Eph. 3:19 that the love of God passes all knowledge.

Sometimes, I see believers struggling to get people baptized in the Holy Ghost. When I turn to diagnose the reason for the struggle and hindrances, I find that the problem is not the anointing; the problem is ignorance. They are trying to get them baptized with the Spirit of God. but the people who are to receive baptism don't have adequate knowledge about the Holy Spirit, its purpose, and the benefits of being baptized in the Spirit.

Why will some, irrespective of their ignorance, still receive the outpouring? This happens due to mercy; the Holy Spirit breaks protocols out of sovereignty. Sometimes, it happens based on the strength of the intercession that carried out for them.

And a certain Jew named Apollos, born at Alexandria, an eloquent man, and mighty in the scriptures, came to Ephesus.

"This man was instructed in the way of the Lord; and being fervent in the spirit, he spake and taught diligently the things of the Lord, knowing only the baptism of

John. And he began to speak boldly in the synagogue: whom when Aquila and Priscilla had heard, they took him unto them, and expounded unto him the way of God more perfectly". — Acts 18:24-26 KJV.

When you check Acts 18:24–26, you will see a certain man named Apollos. He was instructed in the ways of God, mighty in scriptures, but he only knows about the Baptism of John; he is not aware of the Baptism of the Holy Spirit, but the moment Aquila and Priscilla guided him in verse 26 of Acts 18. He was baptized (Acts 19:1–7).

Chapter 11

BENEFITS OF HOLY GHOST BAPTISM

The baptism in the Holy Spirit is a profound spiritual encounter that enriches the believer's life in numerous ways. Here, we explore ten key benefits:

Power to Witness Effectively

"But ye shall receive power, after that the Holy Ghost is come upon you: and ye shall be witnesses unto me both in Jerusalem, and in all Judaea, and in Samaria, and unto the uttermost part of the earth." (Acts 1:8).

The Holy Ghost empowers believers with the ability and tremendous power to be an effective witness of Jesus Christ. This power transcends natural abilities, enabling believers to share the Gospel with conviction and impact.

Prayer Language

"For he that speaketh in an unknown tongue speaketh not unto men, but unto God: for no man understandeth him; howbeit in the spirit he speaketh myste ries... He that speaketh in an unknown tongue edifieth

himself; but he that prophesieth edifieth the church."
1 Corinthians 14:2, 4 (KJV).

Holy Ghost Baptism provides believers with a prayer language
to communicate with God, bypassing human limitations. This
personal prayer language that enhances personal edification and
fosters deeper communion with God.

Supernatural Prayer Abilities

> "Likewise the Spirit also helpeth our infirmities: for
> we know not what we should pray for as we ought:
> but the Spirit itself maketh intercession for us with
> groanings which cannot be uttered. And he that
> searcheth the hearts knoweth what is the mind of the
> Spirit, because he maketh intercession for the saints
> according to the will of God." Romans 8:26-27
> (KJV).

The Holy Spirit assists us in our weaknesses, especially in
prayer, by interceding for us in ways that align with God's will,
enabling us to pray effectively even in situations where we are
unsure of what to pray for.

Activation of God's Deposit Within Us

> "And when Paul had laid his hands upon them, the
> Holy Ghost came on them; and they spake with
> tongues, and prophesied." Acts 19:6 (KJV).

Holy Ghost Baptism stirs the gifts and callings of God that lie dormant within believers, bringing them to life.

Impartation of Spiritual Gifts

"Now concerning spiritual gifts, brethren, I would not have you ignorant. Ye know that ye were Gentiles, carried away unto these dumb idols, even as ye were led. Wherefore I give you to understand, that no man speaking by the Spirit of God calleth Jesus accursed: and that no man can say that Jesus is the Lord, but by the Holy Ghost. Now there are diversities of gifts, but the same Spirit. And there are differences of administrations, but the same Lord. And there are diversities of operations, but it is the same God which worketh all in all. But the manifestation of the Spirit is given to every man to profit withal." 1 Corinthians 12:1–7 (KJV).

It comes with the impartation of a spiritual gift. Believers are endowed with various spiritual gifts to benefit the church, fostering unity and diversity in service to God.

Increased Sensitivity to the Holy Spirit

"But strong meat belongeth to them that are of full age, even those who by reason of use have their senses exercised to discern both good and evil." (Hebrews 5:14). "For as many as are led by the Spirit of God, they are the sons of God" Romans 8:14 (KJV).

The baptism in the Holy Spirit enables us to be more sensitive to the Holy Spirit. The baptism enhances spiritual discernment, making believers more attuned to the promptings and guidance of the Holy Spirit.

Clearer Revelation of Scripture

"Howbeit when he, the Spirit of truth, is come, he will guide you into all truth: for he shall not speak of himself; but whatsoever he shall hear, that shall he speak: and he will shew you things to come." John 16:13 (KJV).

The Holy Spirit enables us to have a clearer revelation of God's words.

Mysteries Spoken to God

"For he that speaketh in an unknown tongue speaketh not unto men, but unto God: for no man understandeth him; howbeit in the spirit he speaketh mysteries... 14. For if I pray in an unknown tongue, my spirit prayeth, but my understanding is unfruitful" 1 Corinthians 14:2,14 (KJV).

Through Holy Ghost Baptism, we speak mysteries to God. This benefit emphasizes the unique communication channel with God that speaking in tongues provides, through which mysteries of the divine are expressed.

Indwelling of the Holy Spirit

"What? know ye not that your body is the temple of
the Holy Ghost which is in you, which ye have of God,
and ye are not your own?" 1 Corinthians 6:19 (KJV).

The baptism in the Holy Spirit confirms the believer as a living
temple of God, where His Spirit dwells continually.

Unction for Kingdom Service

"But the anointing which ye have received of him
abideth in you, and ye need not that any man teach
you: but as the same anointing teacheth you of all
things, and is truth, and is no lie, and even as it hath
taught you, ye shall abide in him." 1 John 2:27 (KJV).

Through Holy Ghost Baptism, we receive unction to become
effective for various forms of service in God's kingdom.

Chapter 12

More Books By Felix Domrufus

- Stages of Spiritual Growth

- 100 Works of the Holy Spirit in the Life of a Believer

- Gifts of the Holy Spirit

- The Ministry of the Holy Spirit

- Secret of Retentive Memory

*L*ook *for these titles in stores and online soon!*